The Drawings of Bertrand

THE DRAWINGS OF

RAYMOND BERTRAND

with an introduction
by
Emmanuelle Arsan

Grove Press, Inc.

Introduction

PISTILS OR STAMENS:

The Promise of a Gala Occasion

Erotic art is our way of enjoying ourselves above and beyond our condition. Art is thus led back to its first purpose, which is to surmount the baseness of matter and to inspire respect for pure chance.

Sensual fantasy is perhaps the only flowering of space and time that can forget its obsessive concern for the fact that its days are numbered, as well as the grief occasioned by its physical dependency, by erecting a universe of non-natural forms that defies nature. The earth it promises us is pre-Euclidian, anti-Riemannian, post-Einsteinian. It peoples this earth with creatures drawn from its own seared brain and rashly fills the emptinesses that existence leaves in man. Disdainful of uncrossable lines, passing through the meshes of the possible, it takes us away to those much-desired places where we can wait for knowledge to catch up with us without too great a feeling of boredom or impatience.

Happiness is the end-product of these multitudes of impulsive acts and intimate feelings of pride, out of which, ever since the days of bone and rock, each and every work, whether a great one or a futile one, has emerged. The joy of the creator stems not so much from having done something, as from having done it outside of the usual molds and contrary to the rules. His triumph is to have gone from the status of a plaything to that of a player, mocking the established order of things.

Art is what is produced when the infinitely extensible laws of genuine pleasure replace the infinitely limited laws of the real. This transmutation is exactly the same as the movement whereby sex becomes genius by refusing to limit itself to the deadly banalities of the discipline of reproduction.

Art is therefore erotic in and of itself. It may sometimes be beside itself, but even the artist who paints virgins or apples does not succeed in fooling us about his motives: their skin of paint or watercolor is an erogenous flesh that evokes the artist's hand in a state of erection. There is no difference between a madonna by Fra Lippo Lippi and a plate of fruit by Cézanne, other than that between two possibilities of orgasm that our brain envisages.

The only difference, in short, between art that admits that it is erotic and art that protests that it is not erotic is frankness. If this world is governed by the good, this ought to be enough to make the one a virtue and the other a perversion. Since our species is moral, any other opinion could be nothing but the result of a passing fancy.

Things will be put to rights sooner if the tedious quarrel between art and beauty (which is recent, but already seems to have been going on for a long time) comes to an end.

Art, of course, is the beginning of the surreal and cannot be anything else — but what is beauty if it is not surreality itself? Beauty is not in nature: it is the least natural find of the mind of man.

To resent beauty for the services it has rendered to established hypocrisy and deception is to confuse it with the fallen bark, the dead skins, and the empty shells that it has left behind. Beauty lies not in what is remembered from the past, but in what is about to be done; it lies not in sanctuary but in sacrilege.

Memory is made up of our dead footprints. The bodies that we have loved are as real as our finite number of chances. All the women of yesteryear are ugly.

The body is beautiful only if it is invented. Beauty is the image about to be conceived, which will forever outmode all the carapaces and girdles of yesterday. The bodies that we are capable of loving have not yet been imagined. They are what the irrational wishes that give our senses power will make them. Their successive mutations will little by little bring us closer to a universe that will serve us.

The beloved mistresses that we dream of anticipate our dreams and advance all by themselves along the asymptotic axes of that imaginary space which is the only landscape that we do not tire of. Today's women would already be old-fashioned to us and we would merely see them growing older and older if they were not intuitively aware of the future moltings which will be the source of our changing ideas of beauty. Those who seem most beautiful to us are those who are proceeding fastest in the direction that we intuit without saying so. They have the blackest eyelashes, the palest mouths, the longest hair, the shortest skirts, and make all women who are guided by the dimensions of their time invisible.

Thus art and the future body of women are closely allied in the search for beauty. Like Artaud's world, the body is yet to be fashioned; it has not yet been found. And it is more difficult to invent it than to construct on paper the abstract beauty of forms as yet unseen. The invention that requires the most genius is that of a beauty that we think we recognize.

If we dream only disincarnated dreams, does the "somewhere out of this world" that becomes ours make us feel any less at home than the beauty of our own species when the extravagance of the artist once again turns it over to the marvelous? And now that the formless and the hideous have become familiar to us, doesn't surrealism consist of rediscovering what unheard-of things beauty can bring us?

The subversion of nature has thus been kindled anew; it is more disturbing than ever in the new generation of madmen for whom the inspiration of surrealism stems more clearly from the foretaste of women of the future than from the dismembering of past uglinesses. The fabulous sources of creative madness will not dry up so long as an exquisite pair of female masturbators abolishes the somatic present of ordinary housewives.

A lucid obsession with beauty, a concrete vision of the immanence of metamorphoses, an autoerotic monosexual power of sensual enjoyment: these characteristics give one newcomer a prominent place among these makers of realizable dreams, a newcomer whose work, barely begun, already excites us as much by its abundance as by its clarity. Besides, if he were not young and in a hurry, would we pay any attention to him? We do not have the time to take an interest in the farewells of those who are deader than we are.

Forgetfulness blossoms everywhere in the world without a background in which Bertrand makes us lose our way. We breathe it in with the wind and the pollen, in the scent of petals on a summer morning. The efflorescent bodies that he draws out of an invisible humus are the only nature that we belong to here. If we did not fuse with them in a passion that has no memory, what other incarnations would we be capable of?

As long as the magic spell lasts, the women that we should like to be will spring up naked from the integument of plants, already barely remembering having been grass or seaweed. Their molting will bare us to the birth of seasons like new creatures. Our breasts will savor their first tumescences as young seedlings. Our fingers will learn to split our arching trunk in order to engraft their artful shoots in it. Thus no sunrise will find us the same as before, from graft to graft: every pleasure will make us put out a fresh bud, every slumber of our memories will cover us with new branches. The imaginary genes that our sap carries will tirelessly deliver us over to the formula of change. We will be happy.

Or is it to defend us against excessive faith that Raymond Bertrand takes such meticulous care to arouse our hopes and then disappoint them? The wide-open gazes that he gives his amorous algae—gazes more transparent than any pearly sheen beneath their innocent eyelashes—have only themselves as their object. The flaring nostrils, the pouting, already swollen lips, the careless poses are there, doubtless, to make us realize that our pleasures cannot concern the absent souls of these complete strangers.

But what exactly have they come to teach us? It will

surely help us to discover what it is if we attentively contemplate their breasts, more supple and resilient than any earthly flesh, their symmetrical nipples starred by infinitesimal cross-hatches and surrounded, without a single break in their botanical eyelashes, by little involucres suggestive of sensual pleasures that are better ordered and more precise than those our imperfect species is capable of.

What touches us more than all this precise fiction, however, are the lines that bear witness to childhood ardor: the visible ribs, the shadowy navels, the hips that have the softness of a satisfied pubis, and the inhumanly virginal power of the sex organs. These sex organs, in fact, are the most fascinating invention of this inventor of new desires. Their beauty stems from the fact that it is extraverted, recalling nothing of our gaping slits and humid mucous membranes, ready to yield beneath the thrust of the possessor. Conscious of what they want and mistresses of the way they prefer to attain sexual climax, their solid and neatly outlined mouths, as circular and as prominent as the vigorous boles of a young tree, do not allow themselves to be penetrated: they are what comes forward and closes around the object of their covetousness. Because of their unusual form and self-assurance, we intuit similar prodigies within the depths of these bodies that are free of our perverse sublimations.

This spare rigor has more power and originality than

the fantasy in which the artist at other times (though he may give this up later) yields to the temptation to transform bellies into faces, to study the changes of expression of a vampire. It is when they give up any sort of props, stop piercing themselves with needles and nails, with pikes and stakes, and no longer lace themselves into tight corselets or suck the sugary sweetness of an ear of corn from a sly sex organ that Bertrand's serene girls seem to us to be most clearly endowed with enviable powers. If we pardon the witches their brooms and the fisherwomen their rushes, it is because the pure joy in their eyes confounds us more than their magic spells.

Why should we be astonished if dildoes, even ones made of plants, look somewhat incongruous on these harmonious Eves whose ambiguity is sufficient unto itself? The stockings of sepals or the willow that they peel off in order to be more naked, the leaves, the lianas and the brambles, the sponges and the madrepores which coif them with their debauchery are rather erotic attributes. And we are borne off to a more equivocal universe—by a coleopter-Cleopatra whose breasts, wings, and eyes match each other, by the tongue stuck out by an archangel with the long venomous eyelashes of a jellyfish, by arching loins that escape their arborescent tunic or their chrysalis —than the one to which we are transported by the fetters that bind breasts and buttocks too gently for us to take the sadistic liturgies of the artist seriously. This is not the environment in which he is most comfortable; his personality is more at ease when he prowls the limits of the different kingdoms, where the frontier between animal, vegetable, and mineral is not very clearly defined and the viewer does not know what language to trust to describe the teguments and the antennae, the polyps and the mosses, the coats of fur and the pigments, the wings and the cuirasses whose enigmatic debris adheres to the pink skin of truncated women (how is one to know how long this has been so, or how long it will continue to be so?). And when a sudden cross-section or the opening of their bodies reveals that their insides are made, not of muscles and nerves, viscera and blood, but rather of a savory abundance of berries, currants, and grapes, the pearly drops that measure out their pleasure for us inspire more rash projects in us than any crucifixion or any so-called phallic penetration.

Is there anyone, moreover, who does not see that the male has very little place in Bertrand's work? Except when a phantasmagorial acorn (one made, however, of involuted leaves) invades an entire abdomen and is outlined in graceful symbiosis beneath the woman's skin, the rarity of male symbols is almost shameful. If a giant mask is perhaps one of them, it is filling the round sex of a nymph with fruitlike breasts and the luminous skull of the telepath with an asexual tongue. In any case, there is another woman at the controls inside the fraudulent lover.

If one looks closely, the only unquestionable male symbols in the world born of an unexplained quirk of Evolution are those mimicked by feminine thighs and buttocks. At the end of his avatars, man is made only of the bodies of women, and this is not the least interesting piece of news offered us. Bertrand would not teach us so much about the subject were he not also a Lesbian.

In a simple work in which all we see is two heads with anemone hair resting one against the other, we must believe that a quite unusual passion has guided the hand of the artist for us to be able to feel such expectant pleasure behind the apparent calm of the scene. But when buttocks contract while nothing else moves, when two tongues find each other deep inside two mouths and two rounded bodies swell as softly as fledglings, when a back curves over knees whose presence we intuit, we truly understand that Bertrand wants to tell us this above all else.

It is not simply talent that gives the shadow traced by his pencil to represent the partial crushing of a breast being penetrated by another amorous breast the power to make us hear the moaning of the two women making love. The sexual happiness that rims the lips and closes the pupils of the other woman whose practiced fingers satisfy the sex of her beloved or who stands and plays with her like a 'cello have been represented by an artist who feels this to be the essence of happiness.

The embrace of girls above whom a slipknot hangs suspended is more troubling. Is it an allegory of their precarious joy? Or will two of them pass this rope around the neck of a third at any moment? The truth is that the beauty of their downy backs and their round buttocks, the ecstasy of the breast swelling between the lips that suck at it is more important to us than what is going to happen. Our good fortune, and their rapture, in any case, will never end as long as our gaze perpetuates the perfection of this charming inflorescence. The wish of the poet suspends the destiny of mortal kisses. <u>Halt, moment, thou art so beautiful!</u>

There is authentic eroticism in this predilection of a man for loveplay from which his sex is absent. Who is ignorant of the fact sapphism is the <u>fabulous wish</u> of men who love women to the point of losing their minds over them—because it multiplies the number of beloved women more infinitely than fornication or mirrors, and peoples the world of the beauty of love with them alone? The artist must be possessed of little esthetic delicacy, in fact, if he allows a man's discordant form to mar a masterpiece of virgins enfolded in each other's arms, unmindful of a vulgarity that causes stupid torturers to enforce the dismal animal law of genres by applying negative categories and antiquated holdovers from grammar.

"Her spirit," Bertrand writes of one of his creatures, "is a castle where human dogs in gold and silver metal slumber." May he forgive us if we don't believe a word of it: the women that he brings forth from his brain and to whom he gives a beauty never seen before on this earth do not have such inner defenses and such outmoded tastes. It is revealing that the ithyphalluses of twisted leaves *that they were for a moment adorned with now no longer concern them, since they tear away these simulacra the moment that the adoring mouth of their beloved approaches their sex. But there is also something else to be said about them: there is no place for anything perverse or abnormal in their world.*

In the place that they have reached—the place where Bertrand has led them, apparently, without knowing it—the mind knows neither walls nor guardians: it knows only the blank white rectangles in the background, with nothing to date them and enclose them, against which the purity of the fearless dreams that we have the strength to dream appears in the light of eternal day.

If others think it important, let them emphasize what Bertrand owes to Leonor Fini or how he differs from Molinier and many others. This knowledge will in no way change the delight that takes hold of us when, even though we like the work of these painters, we nonetheless make a place for Bertrand in our taste. Perhaps this is because we foresee that he has just begun to astonish us and that what he manages to invent in the future will be so strange and so profuse that it is better for us women to immediately prepare ourselves to fall in love frequently.

Emmanuelle Arsan
—Translated by Helen R. Lane

Bertrand

R. Bertrand 68

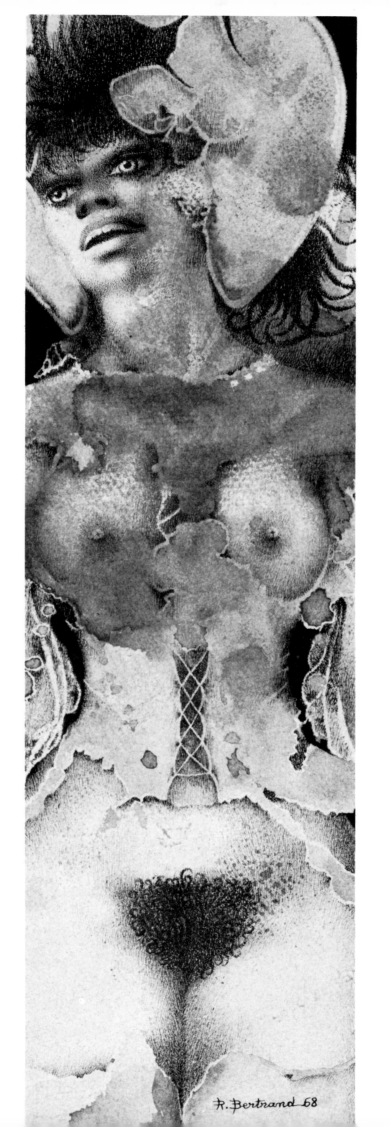

R. Bertrand__68.

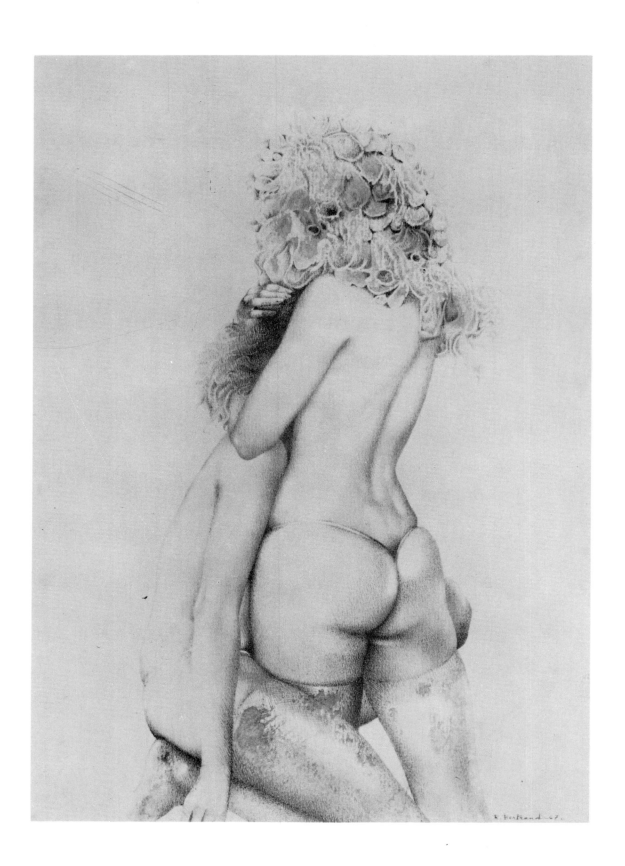

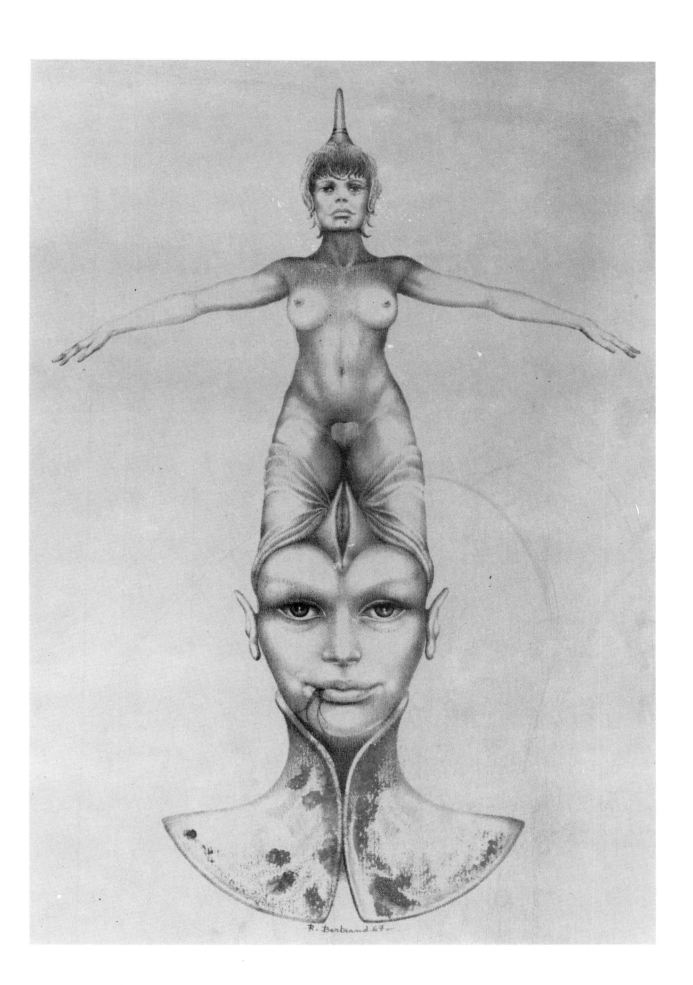

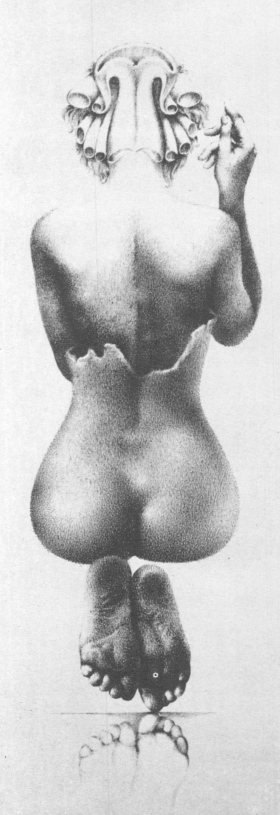

R. Bertrand 68

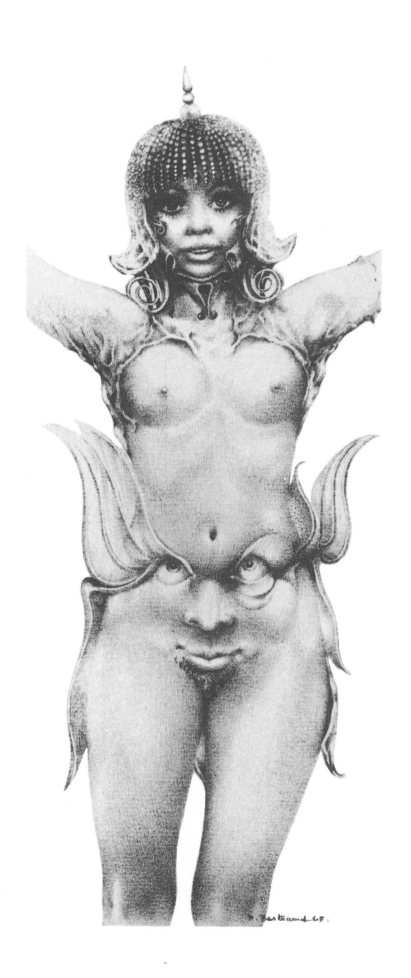

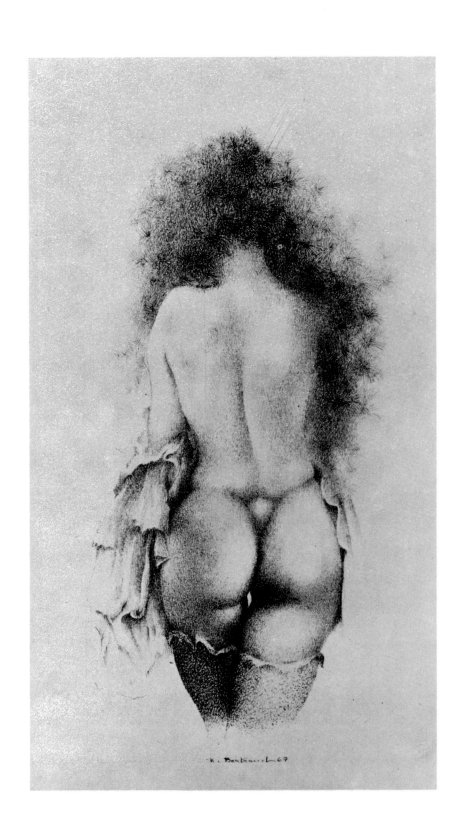

R. Bertrand - 68 -

my darling my darling my darling my darling

- R. Bertrand 68 -

R. Bertrand 68.

Paintings

R. Bertrand 69

R. Bertrand 69

A. Bertrand 63

R. Bertrand 68.

R. Bertrand 68

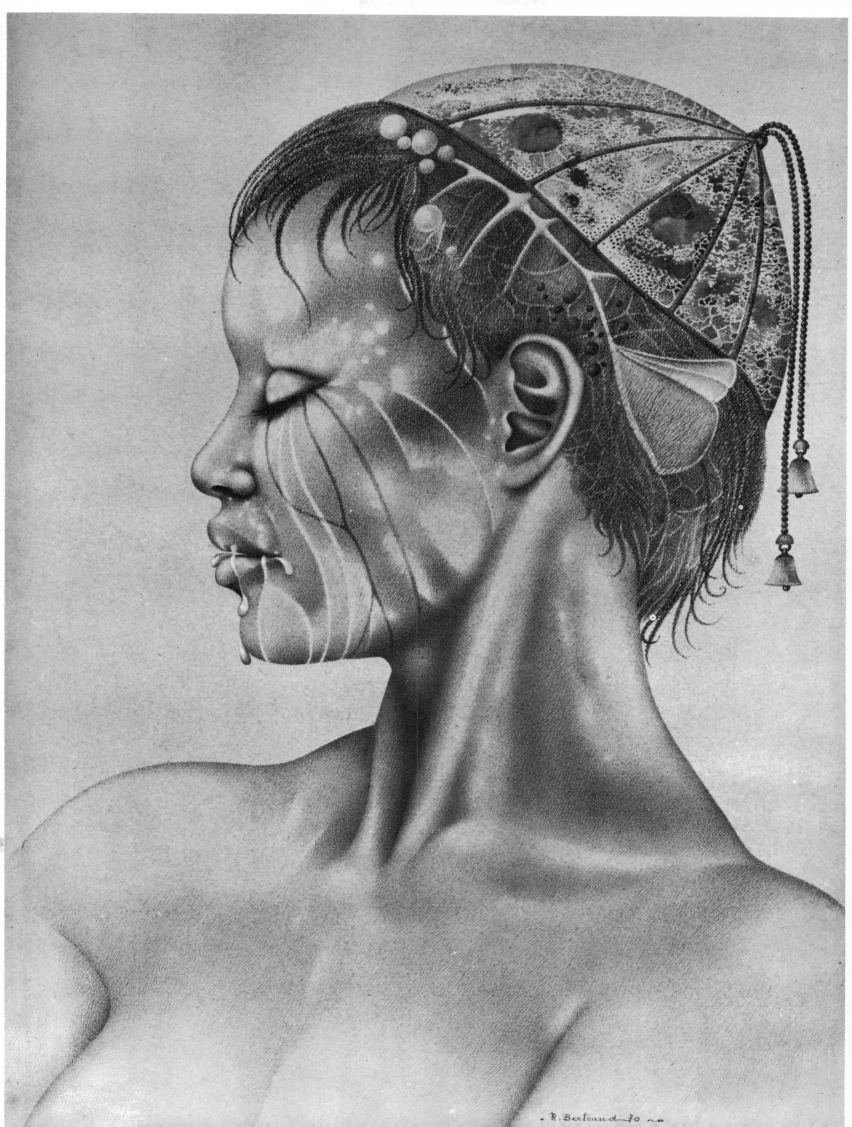

R. Bertrand 70

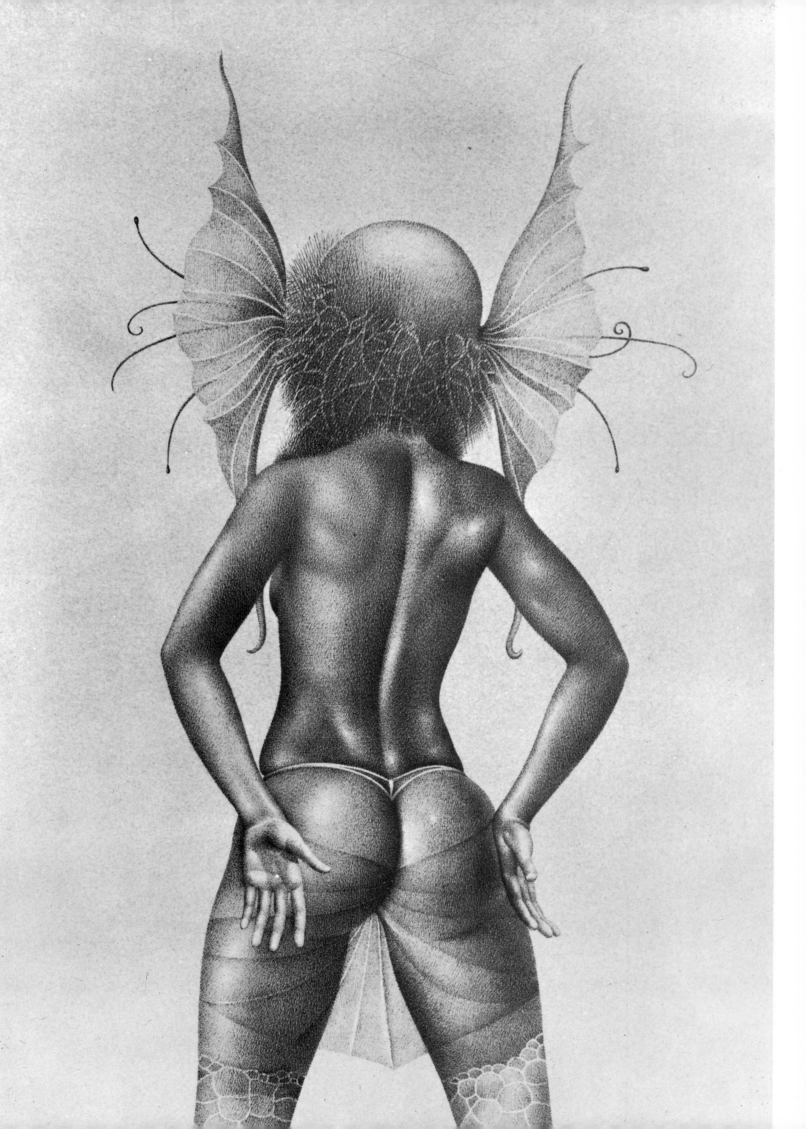